HOW 2 BEE YOUR BEST SELF!

HOW 2 BEE YOUR BEST SELF!

101 Ways 2 Be Your Best Self, Really!

Ed Cawley

How 2 Bee Your Best Self
Copyright © 2020 by Ed Cawley

Self-Help

Library of Congress Control Number: *2020915577*
ISBN-13:   Paperback: *978-1-64749-217-5*

All rights reserved. No part of this publication may be reproduced, distributed, or transmitted in any form or by any means, including photocopying, recording, or other electronic or mechanical methods, without the prior written permission of the publisher or author, except in the case of brief quotations embodied in critical reviews and certain other noncommercial uses permitted by copyright law.

Although every precaution has been taken to verify the accuracy of the information contained herein, the author and publisher assume no responsibility for any errors or omissions. No liability is assumed for damages that may result from the use of information contained within.

Printed in the United States of America

GoToPublish LLC
1-888-337-1724
www.gotopublish.com
info@gotopublish.com

Contents

Chapter One: Know Thyself 9

Chapter Two: Choose Wisely 21

Chapter Three: Strive for Success 31

Chapter Four: Be Money Smart 37

Chapter Five: Use Your Hands 55

Chapter Six: Health Matters 63

Chapter Seven: Love Unashamedly 73

Chapter Eight: Cultivate Your Creative Spirit 77

Chapter Nine: Take the High Road 83

Foreword:

I have been writing this book for over 20 years. I have spent thousands of hours reading books, articles, and information on the Internet about personal development, motivation, and self-help ideas and concepts. One day I realized that all of these approaches were missing some of what I considered to be fundamental tenants of what was needed for a person to survive in a civilized society.

I started to write them down, but everyday life, as so often happens, got in the way. There were planes to catch and bills to pay, so I wound up thinking about my book, coming up with a few precepts occasionally, but not taking the time to write many of them down for a number of years.

Finally in 2012 I figured that whether the Myans got it right about the world ending in 2012 or not, I needed to finish my book.

I would like to thank my wife, Florence Cawley, who has always encouraged me to indulge my creativity, whether it is performing on stage in Community Theater, writing music, playing my guitar, or writing one of the several books and plays I have started but never finished.

So, without hesitation, I present to you:

HOW 2 Bee Your Best Self

Chapter One

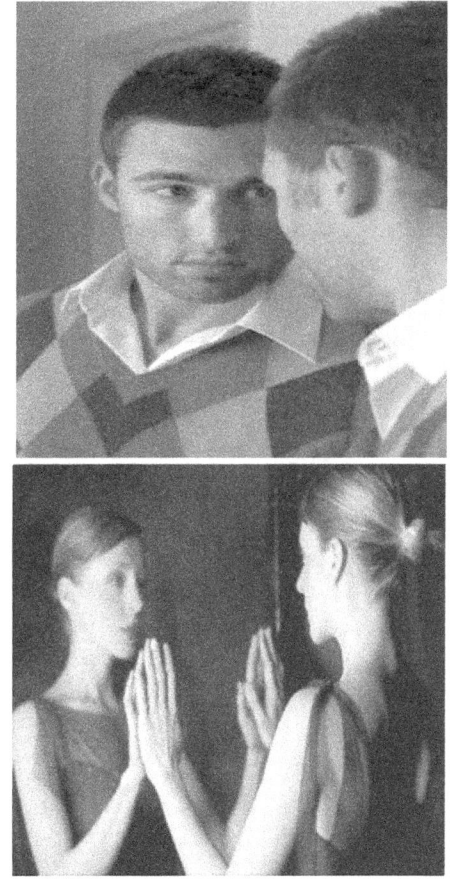

Know Thyself

1. Never lie to the **Person** in the mirror.

Do not deceive yourself into believing you are someone you are not. There is an old saying that goes, "You can fool some of the people all of the time and all of the people some of the time, but you cannot fool all of the people all of the time." However, you should never mislead yourself at any time.

Only if you accept who you are, can you take the steps necessary to improve yourself.

You may occasionally lie to someone else if you do so with a generous spirit. "No, that dress looks great on you, Baby; your butt looks fine!"

Still, you should never lie to the person who looks back at you from the mirror. Self-delusion is a trap and can spiral into a life lost.

The Genie in Aladin got it right, "BEE Yourself." You can't be anyone else, but you can become the best you can bee.

2. **Always strive to be a better person than you are.**

    Every day is a new opportunity to take that first step towards becoming a superior you.
    At any given moment, if you are unsure of how you are doing, ask yourself if you are doing the best you can do; if the answer is "no," then do better.

3. **If you Believe it, you can achieve it.**

    This is the foundation of the belief system that will allow you to accomplish any goal that you set for yourself.
    If you believe in yourself and believe that you can accomplish anything, then you can.
    You are only being held back by your own fear and insecurity.
    If you don't try at all, you will fail 100% of the time. So, step up to the plate and swing for the bleachers. Give it your best shot. You might be surprised at how often you will succeed.

4. Be independent of both the criticisms and praises of others.

You know yourself better than anyone. Fame is fleeting and not all criticisms are justified. When you are able to accept both praise and criticism and simply say, "Thank you," you will have mastered yourself and your self-image.

Saying "thank you" for praise acknowledges your appreciation for the compliment and the person who gave it to you. If you attempt to be humble and act as if it were nothing, then you have belittled the acclaim and the person who just praised you.

It will be difficult to say "thank you" for being criticized. However, you should not make excuses or assign blame for criticism that may be justified.

If the criticism is justified, then you must do better in the future. If it isn't, then nothing you can say will make a difference anyway. That simply means that the person criticizing you is trying to belittle you and you should ignore the criticism.

5. Be aware of your mental imagery.

You are who you think you are.

If you see yourself as someone who is happy to be alive and walk around with your head held high and your shoulders held back, then that is who you will be.

If you see yourself as someone who, if it weren't for bad luck, you'd have no luck at all and walk around with your shoulders stooped and a hang-dog expression, then that's who you will be.

Either way, others will treat you the way you treat yourself.

6. Realize that you are at once both better and worse than you think you are.

The challenge is in understanding yourself enough to realize which is which.

If you are very good at something be proud but not arrogant. If you are not good at something you want to be better at, do what it takes to become more proficient.

7. Use affirmations to become who and what you want to be.

Affirmations are very powerful positive mental images that you can use to improve yourself.

For example, if you weigh 200 pounds and want to lose weight down to 175 pounds, then you can write an affirmation that states, "I eat only enough healthy foods to keep my body at my optimum weight of 175 pounds." Place this affirmation where you will read it dozens of times throughout the day.

As you read it, you will begin to eat differently, and over time, you will become the weight you want to be.

You can use this method to make significant changes in nearly any aspect of your life.

8.   Know your strengths.

Never let someone else belittle your abilities or define who you are or what you are capable of. Eleanor Roosevelt said it best when she said, "No one can make you feel inferior without your consent."

9.   Be aware of your abilities.

Measure yourself against what you can do that you have not yet done rather than compare yourself to anyone else.

10.   Learn to recognize and embrace your talents.

Try different things: write a story, draw a picture, put together a model, or sing a song. If you find that you have a talent for something, cultivate that activity.

11. Accept your imperfections, but never your shortcomings.

Use these definitions:

Imperfections are things about yourself that you wish you could change, but you really have no control over. Examples are, "I wish I weren't so short, tall, left-handed, etc."

Shortcomings are things that you can change if you choose to spend the time and effort. You can correct things such as, "I wish I weren't so fat, skinny, uneducated, etc."

12. Never talk down to yourself.

Sure, you may not be the sharpest tool in the shed, but you're certainly not the dullest either.

Accept the fact that there are always smarter people than you in the world. However, that fact has nothing to do with you **BEING THE BEST YOU CAN BEE.**

13. Ignore your inner critic.

Your main inner critic is fear. Fear is simply **F**alse **E**xpectations **A**ppearing **R**eal. Frank Herbert was correct when he said, "Fear is the mind killer." Fear can immobilize you.

14. Imagine a different reality.

Don't get caught in a rut of always doing the same things in the same way. Try new things; expand your abilities and your horizons. Step outside of your comfort zone.

However, if you do something in a different way, make sure it is a better way than you did it before. Being different must always lead to being better.

Get creative with your life. You may find that the new talent you discovered was the best thing that ever happened to you.

15. Realize that only you can make you happy.

Other people may do things that please you, but ultimately it is your responsibility to make yourself happy.

Your happiness comes first, but it should never be at the expense of another.

16. Accept the simple fact that some days you are the windshield and some days you are the bug.

Don't take it personally.

The windshield did not set out that day to destroy the bug and the bug certainly did not intend to kill itself for the sole purpose of making the windshield difficult to see out of.

Most of the time, however, the Universe is simply not particularly interested in any specific windshield or bug.

It is up to you to do what you must do in order to make your life better.

17. Embrace your mistakes.

Use your mistakes as learning tools and grow from them. This way you can learn true humility.

18. Accept your humanity but never your prejudices.

We have all been programmed with who we are, who the "right kind of people" are for us, and how we should react to any others who are different.

One of the most difficult tasks we will have is overcoming our childhood brainwashing by well-meaning caregivers. These people weren't trying to make us into bad people, they simply taught us what they had been taught when they were children. They did not really understand that they were teaching the next generation how to be prejudiced.

19. Be the change you want to see in the world.

Never forget that you have the power to change the world, even if it is only in your own special corner of the world.

Stand up for a cause you believe in. Write a letter to the editor of your local paper to address something you think should be done differently. Get involved in causes you feel passionately about whether it is helping less fortunate people or rescuing abused animals.

You may not see an immediate change in what you are trying to accomplish, but little actions can have dramatic results in the long run. You never know what kinds of future events will be triggered by your actions today!

Chapter Two

Choose Wisely

20. Take personal responsibility for your own actions.

Every day you have choices. You can choose to do or not do anything in your life.

No one can make you do anything that you do not agree to do, unless, of course that other person has a gun to your head and is making you open the bank vault.

Short of that, however, no one can really make you do anything. The excuse of saying that someone else "made" you do something implies that you have no control over your actions. If you truly want to BEE your best, then you must be able to control your actions and reactions.

Never just react to a situation, you should always consider your choices and respond appropriately.

21. Remember that all actions have consequences.

For example, you can choose to get up and go to work or not. If you choose not to go to work, then you must accept the consequences of your actions. Those consequences could be the loss of that job, the loss of a place to live, or the loss of providing for your family.

Every day, millions of American's wake up and go to work at a job they dislike because they have financial responsibilities to themselves and more importantly, to their families.

These people are heroes and deserve respect and admiration.

22. Choose to work.

If you chose to get up and go to work, then you have agreed to do the work assigned by your employer for the pay you have agreed to accept.

You should never badmouth your employer unless you are prepared to leave and find another job.

No employer will tolerate a negative employee for very long.

You need to bloom where you are planted and to strive to bee the best flower in the garden.

23. Give a day's work for a day's pay.

Once you are at your job, you must give it your best. Since you have agreed to accept your employer's money in exchange for your time, you should strive to be the best at whatever your tasks might be. Be aware that these tasks probably will not always be fun, exciting, or challenging, but you need to do them anyway.

This doesn't mean that you should do anything illegal or unethical, but if you have been hired to clean toilets, make sure that you clean them to the best of your ability.

If you want a perfect example of this concept, check out the latrine scene from, "No Time for Sergeants," starring the late Andy Griffith on YouTube and see how he cleaned the latrine. Don't feel compelled to make your toilet seat salute; this example is just for illustration.

24. Keep learning.

Just because you have a low-paying job doesn't mean that you should have no ambition. Go to college or a trade school to improve your likelihood of acquiring and maintaining a better job than you currently have.

Education is a lifelong endeavor. You actually learn things all of the time. If you are going to be learning anyway, get college or vocational credits for learning, so you can get a better job, or perhaps a raise. Find courses that will lead to professional certifications or a marketable degree.

After you have earned as many degrees as you think are necessary, feel free to take courses that feed your soul such as art or music.

You can also take courses in subjects that simply help you understand the world and your place in the world.

Chapter Three

Strive for Success

31. Appreciate that Success is its own reward.

Learn to appreciate a job well done even without the applause of others.

You should be able to look at your own handiwork with quiet pride and a sense of accomplishment. You should not feel the need to consistently parade yourself around for the praises of others.

In your personal success story, determination and perseverance are more important than intelligence and ability.

32. Remember that if things were easy, everyone would be doing it.

You need to understand the 80/20 rule. Twenty percent of the people make eighty percent of the money because they get up earlier, work harder, and work smarter.

Eighty percent of the people only make twenty percent of the money simply because they don't consistently do what it takes to become successful.

You need to make the decision to be in the top earning twenty percent group and take the steps necessary to accomplish it.

33. Be the kind of leader you would follow.

As a leader you should always expect more of yourself than you expect of others. You should never ask someone else to do something you would not do yourself if you have the skill.

You need to strive to catch other people doing the right thing rather than look for mistakes.

You should never use financial or physical advantage to demean others.

34. Listen to the opinions of others.

Listen to other people, but do not blindly follow anyone else's advice. You should carefully consider all options and make a rational decision.

However, you must be open to the possibility that someone else actually knows more about the subject than you do.

35. Never be jealous of someone else's success.

You have the same number of hours in a day, week, month, or year as every other person on earth.

Learn how they became successful. Imitate them to become successful yourself, but never lose who you are.

Besides, it might be that they are not as successful as they seem to be. For example, their success could be an illusion because they are living way beyond their means.

Another possibility is that their success has cost them something else that you consider more valuable. Their business success may have cost them their family relationships. Such a loss of family may not be something you would want to give up.

36. Recognize that success is the best revenge

As you go through life, you will sometimes be the object of unfair treatment by others.

Since it is not socially acceptable to assassinate anyone, you can remove yourself from the situation. You can then become successful in a different endeavor despite the unfair treatment you received in your former workplace.

If you were unfairly terminated from a job, consider it to be an opportunity to find a better job that serves your higher purpose. Your new job might make your heart sing because you may feel better about what you do on a daily basis.

Just don't let any negative situation define who you are.

The adage that if one door closes, another one opens is true. However, you have to recognize the opening door and be willing to choose a different path if you need to.

Sometimes opportunity knocks very softly, and you have to listen carefully or you might miss it.

Chapter Four

Be Money Smart

37. Learn how money works.

Make sure that you understand some critical financial concepts, such as the power of compound interest and the rule of seventy-two.

Money will double if the number of years times the interest rate equals 72. For example, $10,000 at a 7.2% interest rate for 10 years will become $20,000. Do the Math.

Another key concept is understanding opportunity costs. Opportunity costs simply means that choosing to spend money on one thing eliminates the opportunity to either save the money or spend it on something else. Whenever possible, you should consistently choose to spend less and save more.

38. Balance your checkbook every month

Banks make mistakes. Use a computer-based checkbook system for your checkbook.

This way you can categorize your expenses as you go along to see where your money is going.

This record keeping will make doing your taxes much easier.

39. Do your own taxes.

You need to realize that every family is a business. As such, the more you work on your own business of the family, the more you will understand how to keep track of your income and control your expenses.

Get a tax preparation software program and use it to help organize the information that the IRS expects to find in your return.

As long as the IRS will let you, file a paper copy, rather than file electronically. According to research, this will reduce your chances of being audited.

Let the IRS deposit your money into your bank account. This way no one can try to steal your refund check from your mailbox.

40. Never cheat on your taxes.

Dolly, the Dalmatian, may have cost you $2,000.00 in Vet bills this year, but you still can't deduct her as a dependent. Check what's deductible in your tax preparation program.

If you do cheat on your taxes and get caught, it can cost you penalties, interest, and even potentially jail time.

Besides it was income tax evasion that eventually brought down Al Capone, not murder and racketeering.

41. Make a budget.

You don't need to adhere to a restrictive budget and deny yourself any freedom, but a general budget will help you track where the money goes. Also, keep a record of where you spend your cash. Cash money can easily slip out of your pocket for unnecessary purchases.

More people get into financial trouble because they lose sight of things they really need and just buy what they want.

No one really needs the latest and greatest wall-sized smart TV or home entertainment system. This is especially true if you are already having trouble making the rent or mortgage payment.

When in doubt, read rule 46.

42. Always live beneath your means.

It is easy for some people to max out their credit cards and try to show off the affluence that they have not yet achieved. Then, when they lose their jobs or have other financial reversals and can't make their payments, they can go bankrupt.
You are not this person!
You must maintain self-control and a strong sense of self-worth. Do not be pressured by peers and the media to spend what you do not have.

You might begin to fall prey to a very persuasive and entertaining commercial. Then you think you just **HAVE** to break out your credit card and buy this magic pair of running shoes that will make you run twice as fast with no extra training. Oh yeah, like that's going to happen. NOT! You might want to rethink this purchase.

When all else fails take a deep breath and refer to rule 46.

43. Open a savings account for emergencies.

This savings account should have enough money in it to pay your mortgage or rent and utilities for 3 to 6 months.

To get this much money in this account, start by pretending it is a bill to pay and that you have 3 years to pay it. Then divide up the amount of money you will need into 36 easy payments and pay this account first.

If you tap into this emergency account for unexpected expenses, such as an expensive car repair, you need to put the money back as soon as you can. Just start making those easy payments again until the full amount is back in the account.

You need to start saving money even if you still have debt. Pay yourself first and make it automatic is excellent advice that has come down for generations.

44. Start an Individual Retirement Account.

Put as much money as you possibly can into your IRA as soon as you can. After you have your emergency fund in the bank, take that amount that you were paying monthly and place it into your IRA. Just remember that you must have an emergency fund first.

As soon as possible, contribute the maximum amount allowed into your IRA.

Leave your IRA funds alone until it is time to retire; make sure you can't lose any money; make sure you don't pay any fees.

It takes self-discipline and courage to see that money sitting there in your retirement fund and not think of ways to spend it. Many people do not have the self-control to leave this money alone. You must be strong and leave this money alone.

Very few people retire with too much money. Too many people never really retire and are unable to spend their autumn years enjoying their life.

45. Begin a Pre-Tax Retirement savings plan at work.

If you work for a company that has one, contribute to a pre-tax savings plan like a 401(k), a 403(b), or a 457(b). Most large companies offer participation into a 401(k), or if they are a non-profit or government, a 403(b) or a 457(b) pre-tax retirement savings plan.

If your employer offers a match, contribute at least the amount up to the maximum they will match. If they do not match, then simply use this to augment your IRA contributions. Retirement plans such as 401(k)'s and similar plans often have restrictions that your IRA doesn't have.

Every time you get a raise, place this money into your savings plan and continue to live as you did before your raise. Once your IRA contributions have reached the maximum, increase the contributions to your other plans up to the limits allowed.

The same cautions apply; make sure the plan can't lose any money; make sure you don't pay fees; keep it for retirement. Again, almost no one retires with too much money.

46. Develop a disciplined savings attitude.

Remember, it doesn't matter how much money you make. It only matters how much money you keep!

Also, remember to pay yourself first and make it automatic. You should always save at least 10% of your income for your financial future.

Don't wait until you're out of debt to start saving, start saving as soon as you start earning money.

47. Establish credit as soon as you can.

You are only as credit worthy as the credit reporting agencies say you are, so you must control the kinds of information that they collect.

Once a year you can get a free copy of your credit report from the credit bureaus. Use this opportunity to verify the contents and correct any mistakes.

48. Be careful when using a credit card.

Never allow your credit card to be used for splurge purchases and always pay every charge card off every month. Credit card fees and interest charges can really add up.

Read the fine print before you sign the credit card agreement to make certain you understand all of the details.

That exercise machine that you bought on sale and are using for a clothes hanger could wind up costing you more than twice as much as its original price due to the credit card interest that is accumulating on the unpaid balance.

49. Do not loan money to anyone.

Shakespeare got it right. If you loan money to a friend, expect to lose both the money and the friend. If a friend asks for a loan and you can afford it, make it a gift.

If not, then simply explain that you'd love to, but you really can't afford it. If that causes a rift in the friendship, then it wasn't much of a friendship in the first place.

Loans to family members are worse. It's hard for Cousin Ernie to look you in the eye when he knows he owes you $10,000.00 and has no intention of paying it back. Many family rifts occur over borrowed monies.

The only exception to this rule is if you work for a bank or a finance company and you are loaning someone else's money.

50. Establish a good working relationship with a bank.

If you have a savings and/or a checking account at a bank, apply for a credit card through that bank. Ask for a relatively low credit limit such as an amount you could reasonably pay off every month.

Use it for minimal purchases that you would normally use cash or your debit card, such as gasoline.

It is not necessary to have a $20,000 credit limit if you spend $300.00 on gasoline and pay it off every month. Also, if you have established an emergency fund, then you will not need a high limit card for unexpected expenses.

51. Get Cash Back.

Go for the credit card that has the most cash back options. Reward points typically encourage you to purchase things you really don't need just to be able to use the reward points.

Cash back options can reduce your next month's payment or allow you to add to your savings plans.

The exception to only getting cash back is if you can use the reward points to purchase discounted gift cards at stores you normally shop at anyway.

52. Be Credit Smart.

Read rule 46 again. If at all possible, you should save up for any major purchases; however, sometimes you have to balance the necessity of the item, like a car that you must have to get to work, with the need for credit.

Be sure to shop for the money as carefully as you shop for the car.

This would be a great time to use the bank mentioned in rule 50. The car dealer may give you a better price if you already have financing arranged.

53. Invest in yourself.

Money you spend on education is not an expense; it is an investment. As with any investment, if the return on the investment is greater than the cost of investment, then it will be a good investment and borrowing money is a smart thing to do.

However, borrowing money to go to college with no specific career plans and employment potential may not be a good idea.

Your major in 19th century French poetry may not provide employment in a career that will allow you to pay off those student loans that you used the money to party with.

54. Be financially independent of your parents by age 21.

Don't be a KIPPER- **K**ids **I**n **P**arent's **P**ockets **E**roding **R**etirement **S**avings.

Financial Independence may mean working a minimum wage job and living in a tiny apartment with a roommate who is messier than you and doesn't pay their part of the rent.

Financial independence from your parents is especially critical if you have a child. If your child sees you as not living up to your responsibilities, you are teaching that child that it is okay to be lax and irresponsible.

Once your child goes into the real world and compares you poorly to other parents, you will probably lose their respect, which you may never regain.

Children are much more aware than parents think they are. They will remember being hurt, frightened, or lied to for the rest of their lives and may despise you for it.

55. Own your own home.

There is something about waking up in the morning, walking outside, and knowing that this is your home.

If at all possible, pay your home mortgage off before you retire. This is, of course, unless you can use the equity in your home to fund an investment that can guarantee you a rate of return greater than that of the loan.

Walt Disney mortgaged his home to partially fund the original Disneyland. That worked out well, but you probably should not tap into the equity of your home for that investment opportunity for diamond mining in Antarctica you read about on the Internet.

Chapter Five

Use Your Hands

56. Learn how tools work.

You don't need to build a house to learn how a hammer works and that nails can hold things together. Get a how-to book on the use of common tools or take an extension course at your local technical school.

You could just pick up a hammer and start banging at things. Just make sure you don't destroy anything important like your smart phone or computer. When in doubt, refer to rule 58.

57. Buy a set of tools.

Buy one set of good tools that will perform the tasks that you are most likely to have the time and ability to accomplish.

You don't need to spend thousands of dollars for tools that would allow you to work on bulldozers when you drive a Nissan.

However, if you do drive a Nissan, and you want to work on it, you will need a set of metric tools. Learn the difference.

58. Do simple repairs yourself.

You should be able to do simple repairs around the house rather than have to call in an expert for every little thing.

However, you should understand your limitations and know when it is time to call an expert. You don't want to destroy anything beyond repair because you mistakenly thought you could easily fix it.

59. Wash and repair your own clothes.

The concept is pretty simple: put dirty clothes and soap in the washing machine and turn the machine on. After it cuts off, place the clothes in the dryer. When the dryer cuts off, Voila!' clean clothes.

Now you should hang them on a hanger or fold them up. Do it NOW, not in a few minutes, next week, or next year. Clean clothes not put away are just clutter.

If something is torn, fix it now or throw it away. You won't get to it tomorrow, or next week, and un-wearable clothing is also clutter.

60. Learn how to use a needle and thread.

You will find that when using a needle and thread that one indispensable accessory is a thimble. You can start with a travel repair kit found in some hotel rooms.

You can also find a sewing kit where they sell those little bottles of shampoo and mouthwash at Wal-Mart or the Dollar Store.

61. Learn how to iron.

You may decide that it is worth $4.00 or so each to send your dress clothing to the laundry, but you need to understand what it takes to accomplish the task. Besides, you might really need to iron a piece of dress clothing for a special event because you forgot to pick up your laundry.

62. Learn to cook.

No, really! Learn how to use the stove and the oven, not just the microwave and the toaster. You may surprise yourself by actually being able to eat something that you prepared yourself.

Buy a cookbook and try one new recipe a month for a year. Being able to cook for someone else might improve your relationship.

Besides the ability to cook edible food may become important if you have financial problems and cannot afford to eat out.

63. Learn how to read a map.

Learn how to read maps, not just road maps, but a topographical map of the land. You need to understand contour lines and recognize trails and roads.

The closer contour lines are together, the steeper the hill. Trails and roads are marked differently and you need to identify them.

64. Learn how to use a compass.

Understand that the compass points to magnetic north, not true north. If you can both read a map and use a compass, you will be able to do some back country hiking without depending on electronics.

Electronics have the annoying habit of failing at the most inconvenient time. Also, if you drop your GPS device into a stream, do not be surprised that it will stop working. Electronics and water do not get along.

65. Learn basic navigation skills.

You should be able to use the east-west movement of the sun to walk in a northerly direction. You should, at least, be able to recognize the North Star.

66. Understand basic self-defense.

Take a class in self-defense from your local police department or YMCA. Or you could take a karate class.

You don't need to be Bruce Lee, but you should be able to move well enough to protect yourself.

The preference is to be able to diffuse the situation and avoid a physical confrontation if possible. But do not allow yourself to be a victim if you are attacked.

67. Learn how to shoot a gun.

Don't try to be James Bond or Laura Croft. Take lessons on weapon's safety and how to shoot a pistol with a two-handed stance.

You need to become familiar enough so that if the need ever arises, you will feel comfortable handling and using a weapon.

You should never threaten or even point at anyone with a gun, even one that you think is unloaded. Many people have killed their friends with an "empty" gun.

Never leave a gun out where children may find it.

Chapter Six

Health Matters

68. Strive to be healthy.

Make a conscious effort to choose the healthier option whenever presented with choices.

Use the stairs rather than the elevator if you are going up or down less than 10 flights of stairs. Have a low-fat sandwich instead of burgers and fries.

You know what you should do; you just need to do it.

69. Use hand sanitizer.

Use it after you wash your hands, before you handle food, especially food you are going to eat.

If someone around you is coughing or sneezing, use it on the inside of your nose and on your upper lip. A dab in your ears wouldn't hurt either.

It may not protect you completely, but it will certainly help.

70. Understand the concept of optimal health.

You need to understand that the absence of disease does not automatically equate to being in optimal health.

71. Take care of yourself first.

Taking care of your own health is not being selfish. However, if you don't take care of your own health first, then you will not be able to take care of anyone else.

Taking care of your own physical, mental, and emotional well-being will result in your **BEING YOUR BEST SELF.**

It is hard to take care of your loved ones from a hospital bed or mental health facility.

72. Exercise every day.

You don't have to spend 5 hours in the gym or run a marathon every day. You can do just a few simple exercises that will get your muscles firing and your heart pumping.

You don't need to spend a fortune on equipment either. Crunches and push-ups are free and so are walking and running. Just make sure to use proper form.

Be cautious of running on hard surfaces; you don't want to have your knees replaced before you're 50.

73. Learn how your body works.

You need to know what you need to do to help your body remain healthy.

You already know about the fun parts. You should remember something from the basic health class you had in high school.

That's not enough. You need to learn about what happens when you exercise. Be knowledgeable about your basic nutritional requirements and how your musculoskeletal system works to hold your body together.

One useful bit of information is the fact that one pound of fat equates to approximately 4,000 calories. So if you are trying to lose weight, you will need to eat 4,000 calories less than your body needs to maintain your current activity level. Otherwise you will need to increase your activity level to burn an additional 4,000 calories.

You can use any one of the free calorie calculators available on the Internet to find out how best to accomplish your goals.

74. Know your healthy numbers.

Have regular checkups. Know what your blood pressure, blood sugar, and cholesterol levels are. Understand how your height and weight calculate into your Body Mass Index and what those numbers should be in order for you to be considered healthy.

According to the latest medical wisdom, your blood pressure should be 120/80 or slightly lower. If your lower number ever gets over 95, see a doctor.

Blood sugar is the way your body gets fuel for all of your bodily functions. Your blood sugar is measured by the amount of glucose in your blood after fasting. A normal fasting blood glucose level is between 70 and 99 milligram per deciliter of blood, or $1/1000^{th}$ of a gram per $1/10^{th}$ of a liter. Too much sugar can be a sign of diabetes.

Cholesterol is a waxy substance that exists in the blood. It is produced by the liver and found in certain foods. It is needed to make vitamin D and some hormones, build cell walls, and create bile salts that help you digest fat. The amount of cholesterol in the bloodstream is also tested after fasting.

Your total cholesterol should be between 100 and 199 milligrams per deciliter. This breaks down to the three major types; HDL, LDL, and VLDL.

HDL is the good cholesterol and you should have over 39 mg per dL. According to ATP-III guidelines, HDL cholesterol over 59 mg per dL can help reduce your risk of coronary heart disease. LDL is bad cholesterol and you should have an LDL level of under 99 mg per dL. VLDL is very bad cholesterol and you should have no more than 40 mg of VLDL per dL.

Body Mass Index is calculated by your weight in kilograms divided by the square of your height in meters. (kg / m2) A BMI of 18.5 to 24.9 is normal.

75. Be wary of alcohol.

More people are addicted to alcohol than to all other drugs combined. The health benefits purported of having a glass of wine can be achieved by eating fruits and practicing deep breathing.

Social drinking can be a trap if you are not careful. If you ever get so drunk that you can't remember what you did, or you wind up in jail, or some other place that is just as dangerous, stop drinking. Better: don't start.

You don't have to make a big deal out of it by announcing to anyone within earshot of your decision to not drink; just politely decline. A simple "no thank you" should be sufficient.

76. Be careful with over-the-counter and prescription drugs.

Some over the counter medicines do not mix well with prescription drugs. Remember what happened to Heath Ledger. He combined too many O.T.C. medicines and prescription drugs and accidentally killed himself.

Check with your pharmacist for interactions and side effects. You could also do research on the Internet. Unfortunately, not everything on the Internet is accurate.

Also be careful with alcohol and any medication. Pay attention to the warnings on the labels.

When all else fails, read the directions.

77. Never do illegal drugs.

You know the excuses, "everybody's doing them" or "it's just for medicinal purposes." But most illegal drugs have an insidious addictive side that will steal your soul, destroy your mind, and poison your body.

The single most concerning physical effect of taking many illegal drugs is the loss of your ability to make rational judgments. There was an episode of "1000 Ways To Die" when two guys in the woods ran out of marijuana. They decided to pick something else to smoke and picked poison sumac which killed them.

Besides, jail time will not look good on your resume'. Just don't!

Chapter Seven

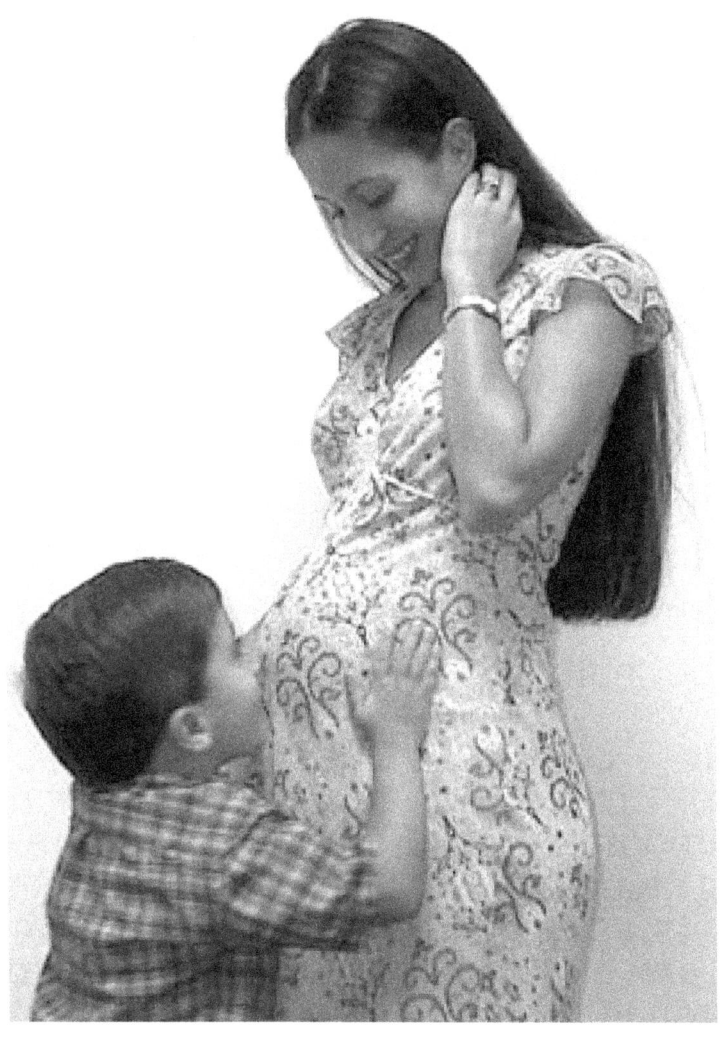

Love Unashamedly

78. **Tell your loved ones that you love them every day.**

There are no guarantees in life and tomorrow may be too late.

Be willing to give them a hug, especially when they need it.

79. **Be willing to ask for a hug when you need it.**

Asking for a hug is not a sign of weakness, but, rather, an acceptance of your humanity. All normal humans require the positive, supportive touch of another human being.

Our current focus on teaching, "good touch-bad touch" is creating a generation of children who are afraid of being touched at all. It is also creating parents, grandparents, aunts and uncles, who are afraid of showing affection to the children in their life.

One has to wonder what the result will be in the future of this tendency not to hug.

80. Listen to your heart.

Your heart will tell you if the object of your affection is someone you want to spend your life with.

Make sure it is your heart you are listening to and not a more selfish body part.

81. Understand Love.

Understand that love is giving and sharing, supporting and caring. Love is waiting instead of hurrying; listening, rather than talking. Love is forgiving, instead of holding a grudge; celebrating, instead of envying. Love is not selfish and controlling.

Obsession and stalking are also not love but forms of mental abuse.

Make sure that you do not mistake another emotion for love or you might find a restraining order keeping you from your imagined true love.

82. Fall in love deeply, madly, truly and completely.

In true love, hold nothing back. Only then can you find real joy.

83. Realize that love is not a means to an end.

You should never use the love of another for you to manipulate that person. Having the love of another is a precious trust.

If you can, return the love. If you can't, at least allow the Golden Rule to restrain your actions.

84. Be more than a frog.

Being a parent has no relationship to having the biological ability to procreate; even frogs have babies.

Don't be a frog; be a responsible parent.

Chapter Eight

Cultivate Your Creative Spirit

85. Nourish your creativity.

Whatever your talent is, spend time cultivating it. You need to spend at least an hour a day working with your creativity.

Failure to do this can lead to depression, despair, and a belief in the futility of life.

86. Be spontaneous not careless.

When you have the opportunity for some unstructured time, make sure it is spent doing something you really enjoy.

Just make certain that you don't do anything stupid like bungee jumping off your 12' garage with a 15' bungee cord.

This decision could also be a result of too much alcohol impairing your ability to make rational judgments.

87. Learn to play a musical instrument.

You will feel immense satisfaction when you play a musical instrument, even if it is just for your own pleasure.

The discipline it takes for you to learn such a skill will translate into the ability to concentrate on any endeavor in life and will enhance your sense of self-worth.

88. Learn to appreciate the artistic endeavors of others.

Go to see a live production of a play. Go to a symphonic or pops concert. Visit an art gallery or museum.

Whether or not your talent is in any one of these fields, you need to understand what it takes to accomplish these feats of creativity.

In this way you will gain a respect for the artists and the art.

89. Log your creativity.

Keep a diary, log book, or electronic recording device close at hand so that if you have an idea, you can record it when you have it. Nothing is more frustrating than trying to remember that idea you had yesterday, and you simply can't remember what it was.

You know it was brilliant, would make you rich, and be a benefit to all mankind, if you could just remember what it was. Dang it!

90. Keep a journal of your life.

You don't need to write something every day, but you should write frequently enough so that as you age, you can look back and understand who you were in different stages of your life.

This journal should NOT be on any kind of Social Media. You do not need to make every move you make public.

In the end, your perception of your life will be the total sum of the memories you made and can recall. Keep good notes; you only pass through here once.

91. Take an intense adventure rather than a relaxing vacation.

Every so often you need to shake things up. Rather than take a week off and go to the beach again, go take a mountain climbing class or survival training course.

You will come back stronger, healthier, and more confident.

Or you could make an adventure goal such as taking a hike in all of the national parks, one at a time. This could be one of your bucket list items.

Chapter Nine

Take the High Road

92. Be the better person.

In every situation in life, be slow to judge. Never be petty or vindictive.

Always pull yourself out and away in order to make decisions from a higher perspective than personal gain.

93. Find solutions to conflicts.

Always try to find the solution to a problem rather than try to find who is at fault. Remember that the one at fault might be you.

94. Be Reliable.

Do what you say you will do when you say you will do it. This way you will establish a reputation for being reliable which will result in earning the respect of others.

95. Be the Peacemaker.

Whether you are in a personal or professional setting, you will inevitably find yourself in the middle of conflicts of one type or another. Other people will be trying to elicit your support for whatever cause or concern they are backing.

Do not let yourself be drawn into the argument. Ask questions and try to calm the situation.

96. Expect everyone to make every mistake once.

Give everyone a second chance; not, a third. Three of the same mistakes indicate a character flaw.

That means that either they are too arrogant to follow guidelines, too ignorant to follow directions, or too careless to want to follow instructions.

97. Be critical, but not harsh.

Criticism should be used only when suggesting a change in the process that would make it better; never, just to find fault.

You should save your strongest criticism for yourself.

98. Never worry.

Do something to resolve the problem or forget about it. Worry never takes the unhappiness out of tomorrow; it just takes the happiness out of today. Besides, worry is simply the fear of the unknown future.

Change the things you can. Accept the things you can't change. This is the Serenity Prayer.

99. Always be ethical in your dealings with other people.

Ethics are what you do when no one is checking up on you. The Golden Rule is the most well-known example of ethical behavior.

100. Be inspirational to other people.

You may think that no one is watching you, but someone always is. Consistently set a good example.

Give praise and recognition to everyone who deserves it. Undeserved praise is hollow and insults the intelligence of the recipient

101. Be observant.

You don't need to be Sherlock Holmes to notice your surroundings and how other people behave.

102. Look for the good in all people.

Realize that not everyone has any.
Once someone has shown their true colors, do not give them a chance to negatively affect you or your family.

103. Be aware of how other people react to you.

You should always strive to be approachable and friendly. You want people to be comfortable around you.
If you sense that they avoid you, maybe it is because you appear distant or unfriendly in some way.
You may want to stand out in a crowd, but you don't want people to think you are a psychopath.

104. Be aware that you can't please everyone; don't try to.

All you can do at any moment is the best you can. If that doesn't please everyone, it has nothing to do with you.

105. Smile.

Even when you don't feel like it, smile anyway. It will improve the way others respond to you and eventually improve your own mood.

106. Don't isolate yourself.

Other people can be a source of inspiration and sometimes amusement.
You are not an island but part of the community of humankind. Embrace the association of others, but be wary. Even the best of friends can become an enemy without you even knowing why.

107. Be respectful to your parents.

They actually had a life before you were born and will have a life when you move out.

Their world only seems to revolve around you because they are patiently waiting for you to live up to at least one of their expectations: that their child has become a responsible adult, not just a very large child with glandular problems.

Don't disappoint them.

108. Care for others and offer help.

Consider that caring for others is not weakness. It is, in fact, one of the hallmarks of being your best self.

There is an old saying, "No man stands as tall as he does when he stoops to help a child." This concept applies to any person helping anyone else who is worse off than they are.

According to Star Trek, the most important 3 words you can say to another person are "Let me help," not "I love you."

109. Be patient.

Have patience with animals and small children; they are probably both smarter than you are.

Have patience with the elderly. They know more than you think they do. They deserve your respect and honor.

110. Be responsible for the care of your pets.

If you have a pet, you have assumed the responsibility for another life. Animals give you unconditional love and companionship. It is your charge to give back care and compassion.

You must never abuse, or neglect an animal. They are dependent on you for food, warmth, medical care, and affection.

The true measure of **BEING YOUR BEST SELF** is found in how you care for animals in your trust.

Pets are not disposable even if they belong to someone else.

111. Give generously.

Just remember that charity begins at home. Be aware that every great philanthropist first had to amass a great fortune before he could be really generous.

Despite the magnanimous generosity of the Bill Gates foundation today, rumors of the cutthroat tactics of Microsoft in the early days still haunt the internet.

Assuming you will probably never be nearly as rich as Bill Gates, you will need to be cautiously generous. Give from your heart, but make sure that you do not give away your ability to pay your bills. Investigate charities to make sure that the primary beneficiaries of the charity are not the people who run it.

Be especially wary of any charity that advertises heavily on television. The odds are that most of their resources go to advertising and administration rather than the causes they claim to benefit.

112. Give to the future of the planet.

Plant a tree that you will never get a chance to sit under.
Contribute to a cause that is greater than yourself.

Recycle when you can.

Leave only your footprints on beaches and in wilderness areas.

113. Practice being quiet.

Turn off your electronics.

If you can't sit and think quietly for 15 minutes without falling asleep, it doesn't count.
You can meditate if you have developed the skill, or pray if you feel so moved, but just being aware of yourself and your surroundings is sufficient.

114. Practice being alone.

Learn how it feels to be really alone—no TV, smart phone, or computer. Imagine, just you, alone somewhere with no one else around and no electronic connection.
Lie on a beach or sit on a rock overlooking a valley. Breathe deeply and enjoy the view.
Reflect on who you are, where you have been, and where you want to go. Don't dwell on negativity, but rather, consider how lucky you are to be right here, right now.

115. Practice being grateful.

Be grateful for every breath you take, for every person in your life, for everything you have, and everything you are.
Not everyone is as lucky as you are and you should celebrate your good fortune.

116. Bee in the present

Ugway said it best. "Yesterday is history, tomorrow is a mystery, today is a gift, that's why we call it the present."
BEE YOUR BEST SELF, today and everyday.